I am so 5!

Sky Pony Press books may be purchased in bulk at special discounts for sales promotion, corporate gifts, fund-raising, or educational purposes. Special editions can also be created to specifications. For details, contact the Special Sales Department, Sky Pony Press, 307 West 36th Street, 11th Floor, New York, NY 10018 or info@skyhorsepublishing.com.

Sky Pony® is a registered trademark of Skyhorse Publishing, Inc.®, a Delaware corporation.

Visit our website at www.skyponypress.com.

Authors, books, and more at SkyPonyPressBlog.com.

10 9 8 7 6 5 4 3 2 1

Library of Congress Cataloging-in-Publication Data is available on file.

Cover illustration and design by John Kurtz

Print ISBN: 978-1-5107-4512-4
Ebook ISBN: 978-1-5107-4515-5

Printed in China

I am so 5!

LOOK AT EVERYTHING I CAN DO!

Sandrina and John Kurtz

Sky Pony Press
New York, New York

I can make music,

and sing,
and dance.

I can button
my shirt,

**and tie
my shoes.**

I can make my own bed,

**and clean up
my room.**

I can do
jumping jacks,

and run backwards.

I can make a
sandwich,

and cut it.

I can write my name,

and read a book.

I can vacuum
the floor,

and make a fort.

I can jump rope,

and play hopscotch.

I can wash my face,

and brush my hair.

I can wait
for my turn,

and slide!

I can nap with my cat,

and teach my
dog manners.

I can make a paper airplane,

and finger puppets.

I can ride my bike,

and balance on
a beam.

I can scavenger hunt,

**and catch
a ball.**

I have friends, new and old.
We are happy, smart, and bold.
It's so much fun to be alive,
because I am so five!